# TOP 10 NFL SUPER BOWL MOST VALUABLE PLAYERS

Ron Knapp

**Enslow Publishers, Inc.**

40 Industrial Road        PO Box 38
Box 398              Aldershot
Berkeley Heights, NJ 07922   Hants GU12 6BP
USA                         UK

http://www.enslow.com

## *Dedication*
### For Ashley Shaw, who loves to read.

**Library of Congress Cataloging-in-Publication Data**

Knapp, Ron.
    Top 10 NFL Super Bowl most valuable players / Ron Knapp.
       p. cm. — (Sports top 10)
    Includes bibliographical references (p. 46) and index.
    Summary: Profiles the lives and careers of Bart Starr, Joe Namath, Lynn
Swann, Terry Bradshaw, Marcus Allen, Doug Williams, Joe Montana, Emmitt
Smith, Terrell Davis, and John Elway.
    ISBN 0-7660-1273-5
    1. Football players—Rating of—Juvenile literature. 2. Football players—
Biography—Juvenile literature. 3. National Football League. 4. Super Bowl.
[1. Football players. 2. Super Bowl.] I. Title. II. Title: Top ten NFL Super Bowl
most valuable players. III. Series.
GV939.A1 K585  2000
796.357'092'273—dc21
[B]                                               99-044903

Printed in the United States of America

10 9 8 7 6 5 4 3 2 1

**Illustration Credits:** AP/Wide World Photos, p. 17; Archive Photos, p. 13; ©
Mitchell Layton, pp. 22, 25, 26, 29, 35, 37, 43; © Mitchell Layton/Newsport,
pp. 33, 38, 41, 45; Green Bay Packers, pp. 7, 9; San Francisco 49ers, p. 31;
Sporting News/Archive Photos, pp. 10, 14, 18, 21.

**Cover Illustration:** © Mitchell Layton/Newsport.

**Cover Description:** Terrell Davis

**Interior Design:** Richard Stalzer

# CONTENTS

# Introduction

**IN THE 1950s,** the National Football League (NFL) was a pretty simple operation. There were twelve teams in two conferences. In late December of each year, the conference winners would meet in the title game. That was the whole postseason.

Then came the American Football League (AFL) in 1960. The new league gained a lot of attention from the media and fans. Both leagues went after the top college prospects. Players such as Joe Namath earned huge contracts in bidding wars between the AFL and the NFL. Also, the new league went after established players. The AFL teams offered big money to NFL stars to switch leagues.

Finally, the older league had had enough. The NFL and AFL agreed to a common draft. They promised to stop trying to sign each other's players. And they agreed to the AFL-NFL World Championship Game, which soon became known as the Super Bowl.

The AFL disappeared in 1970 as its ten teams officially joined the NFL. From then on, the Super Bowl would be the meeting place for the champions of the National Football Conference and the American Football Conference.

After more than three decades, the Super Bowl has become more than just a football championship. It is usually the most watched television event of the year. Advertisers spend millions of dollars to buy a few seconds of commercial time. The attention of the entire country seems focused on the big game—and the elaborate halftime show.

Added together, the athletes in this book have won Most Valuable Player honors in fourteen Super Bowls. All of them are players who regularly handle the ball—five quarterbacks, four running backs, and one receiver.

Three of them, Namath, Doug Williams, and Marcus Allen, played in only a single Super Bowl. That was enough to make sure that they would always be remembered when fans talk about pro football.

The teams that these men were a part of almost always won the Super Bowl. Joe Montana and Terry Bradshaw played in four Super Bowls apiece—and won them all. Bradshaw's teammate, Lynn Swann, also played on four winning teams. Emmitt Smith's teams won three championships, and Bart Starr's two.

John Elway's teams lost three Super Bowls before he and his teammate Terrell Davis became double winners.

Not everyone would agree when choosing ten top Super Bowl MVPs. Perhaps you can think of some others. This is *our* list of the players who have dominated the biggest game in American sports.

## CAREER STATISTICS

| Player | Appearances | MVP |
| --- | --- | --- |
| **BART STARR** | SUPER BOWL I, II | SUPER BOWL I, II |
| **JOE NAMATH** | SUPER BOWL III | SUPER BOWL III |
| **LYNN SWANN** | SUPER BOWL IX, X, XIII, XIV | SUPER BOWL X |
| **TERRY BRADSHAW** | SUPER BOWL IX, X, XIII, XIV | SUPER BOWL XIII, XIV |
| **MARCUS ALLEN** | SUPER BOWL XVIII | SUPER BOWL XVIII |
| **DOUG WILLIAMS** | SUPER BOWL XXII | SUPER BOWL XXII |
| **JOE MONTANA** | SUPER BOWL XVI, XIX, XXIII, XXIV | SUPER BOWL XVI, XIX, XXIV |
| **EMMITT SMITH** | SUPER BOWL XXVII, XXVIII, XXX | SUPER BOWL XXVIII |
| **TERRELL DAVIS** | SUPER BOWL XXXII, XXXIII | SUPER BOWL XXXII |
| **JOHN ELWAY** | SUPER BOWL XXI, XXII, XXIV, XXXII, XXXIII | SUPER BOWL XXXIII |

# BART STARR

**WHEN HE WAS IN JUNIOR HIGH SCHOOL,** Bart Starr did not look like a future football player. He was a small, quiet boy who was not usually noticed. "There he was," said a teammate, "a scrawny kid who couldn't have weighed more than a hundred and five or ten pounds without a football uniform hanging loose all over him."[1]

Starr never got louder, but he did get bigger, stronger, and better at football. When the first-string quarterback broke his leg at Sidney Lanier High School in Lanier, Alabama, Starr took over. He did well enough to earn a scholarship to the University of Alabama.

After spending much of his college football career on the bench, he was chosen in the seventeenth round of the 1956 NFL Draft by one of its worst teams, the Green Bay Packers. In 1959, Vince Lombardi became head coach and eventually made Starr his No. 1 quarterback.

Soon Lombardi's team, with Starr and running backs Jim Taylor and Paul Hornung leading the way, began dominating the NFL. Green Bay won league championships in 1961, 1962, 1965, and 1966.

The 1966 title earned Green Bay a spot in the first AFL-NFL World Championship Game against the American Football League's Kansas City Chiefs. The 1967 match would later become known as the first Super Bowl.

Many fans expected the powerful Packers to dominate the Chiefs, but at halftime Green Bay's lead was only 14–10. However, by then, Starr, who was calling his own plays, had spotted several weaknesses in the Kansas City defense. The Chiefs were having a very tough time covering veteran

**BART STARR**

Bart Starr was one of the greatest on-field leaders in football history. He quarterbacked the Packers to five league championships, including two Super Bowls.

receiver Max McGee. "On a drive of over 50 yards in the third quarter, I hit McGee three times for good gains, the last being a 13-yard post route into the end zone."[2]

McGee caught seven Starr passes that day, totaling 138 yards and two touchdowns. Green Bay won easily, 35–10.

To qualify for Super Bowl II, the Packers had to get past the Dallas Cowboys in the "Ice Bowl," the NFL Championship game, on December 31, 1967. The temperature in Green Bay, Wisconsin, was 13 degrees below zero. A bitter wind brought the wind-chill factor to 40 degrees below zero. "This is crazy," some of the Cowboys whined. "How can you play football in this kind of weather?"[3]

Despite the cold, it was an incredible game. With sixteen seconds left, Dallas led 17–14. Green Bay had the ball on the Dallas one-foot line. There was time for one more play. Starr looked at Lombardi. The coach shrugged his shoulders and pointed at his quarterback. It was up to Starr.

Starr decided he would handle the ball himself. He did not want to risk a handoff in the frigid weather. He told Jerry Kramer, one of his guards, to open a hole and he would follow him into the end zone. Kramer did his job with help from center Ken Bowman—and Starr did too! The quarterback dove over the goal line! Touchdown! Green Bay 21, Dallas 17.

After the Ice Bowl, Super Bowl II seemed anticlimactic. Starr picked apart the Oakland Raiders defense with 13-of-24 passes for 202 yards. The Packers won easily, 33–14.

Even with two Super Bowl MVP trophies, Starr remained a quiet man who did not brag. He knew he had not won all those big games by himself. The Packers did it as a team. "There is respect and admiration among us," he said. "We're forty guys and all forty of us feel that way . . . It may sound a little corny to anyone else. To us it's as genuine as sunshine."[4]

# BART STARR

BORN: January 9, 1934, Montgomery, Alabama.

HIGH SCHOOL: Sidney Lanier High School, Montgomery, Alabama.

COLLEGE: University of Alabama.

PRO: Green Bay Packers, 1956–1971.

RECORDS: Postseason career record for highest passer rating, 104.8; postseason career record for the lowest percentage of intercepted passes, 1.14.

HONORS: Most Valuable Player, Super Bowl I, II; Associated Press regular season MVP, 1966; NFL 1960s all-decade team; elected to Pro Football Hall of Fame, 1977.

After retiring as a player, Starr was the Packers head coach from 1977 until 1983.

**Internet Addresses**

http://www.superbowl.com/history/mvp/sbi.html

http://www.superbowl.com/history/mvp/sbii.html

**JOE NAMATH**

Joe Namath throws a pass. Namath was the first quarterback to throw for over 4,000 yards in a season.

ROCK FIGHTS WITH HIS FRIENDS helped Joe Namath learn to throw hard and straight when he was a kid growing up in Beaver Falls, Pennsylvania. By the time he was a high school senior, he was an All-Star quarterback who had connected on 84 of 120 passes.

At the University of Alabama, Namath played for the legendary coach Paul "Bear" Bryant. He found it hard to follow the rules and got into trouble for gambling and drinking. But in 1964, Namath led the Crimson Tide to the national championship. Bryant called him "the greatest athlete I've ever coached."[1]

When he turned pro after his senior season, two teams, the NFL's St. Louis Cardinals and the New York Jets of the AFL, wanted Namath. A fierce bidding war was finally stopped when the Jets offered him $427,000, an incredible amount of money for an athlete in the 1960s. That was far more than most pro players made in their entire careers. The big contract irritated many fans, players, and reporters.

Namath's unique style alienated many people, too. He had long hair, grew a goatee, and when he was off the field he wore wild and brightly-colored clothing. The title of his autobiography was *I Can't Wait Until Tomorrow . . . 'Cause I Get Better Looking Every Day*.

Namath did not seem to care that many people were cheering against him. He said, "You don't judge a man by the way he cuts his hair."[2] He wanted to be judged by what he did on the football field. What he was doing was turning the Jets into one of the best teams in the AFL. By 1967, Namath had become pro football's first 4,000-yard passer and the Jets were 8–5–1.

His style and accomplishments had made him one of the most well-known athletes in the nation. He was nicknamed "Broadway Joe" after the glittering street in Manhattan. Namath was called "the biggest thing in New York since Babe Ruth."[3]

After an 11–3 regular season in 1968, the Jets earned a spot in Super Bowl III. Namath himself had been one of the reasons the big game had been created in the first place. The two leagues were now in the process of merging. With flashy stars like Namath, the NFL knew the AFL was here to stay. But that did not mean that everybody thought teams in the two leagues were equal. After all, the first two Super Bowls had been one-sided. The NFL's Green Bay Packers had easily beaten Kansas City and Oakland. Why would Super Bowl III be any different? The Baltimore Colts, another NFL powerhouse, were expected to crush the Jets.

Joe Namath had a different idea. "I've got news for you," he announced. "We're going to win this game. I guarantee it."[4] Hardly anybody believed him. Many fans thought he was crazy. Bragging like that might make the Colts angry.

In the game, the Jets defense drove Earl Morrall crazy. He was the Baltimore quarterback who threw three first-half interceptions. Meanwhile, Namath directed a drive that started on his own 20-yard line. Handoffs to Matt Snell netted steady yardage. When the Colts blitzed, Namath hit George Sauer with quick passes. Snell's 4-yard touchdown run made it 7–0 at the half.

Then the Jets got close enough for three second-half field goals. Veteran Johnny Unitas came off the bench and led Baltimore to a touchdown, but time ran out.

Namath ran happily off the field waving one finger in the air. The Jets were No. 1! In the biggest upset in the history of pro football, New York had beaten Baltimore, 16–7.

# JOE NAMATH

BORN: May 31, 1943, Beaver Falls, Pennsylvania.

HIGH SCHOOL: Beaver Falls High School, Beaver Falls, Pennsylvania.

COLLEGE: University of Alabama.

PRO: New York Jets, 1965–1976; Los Angeles Rams, 1977.

HONORS: Most Valuable Player, Super Bowl III; all-time AFL team, 1969; elected to Pro Football Hall of Fame, 1985.

Looking down the field, Namath loads up for a bomb. In Super Bowl III, Namath completed 17 of 28 passes for 208 yards, leading the Jets to an improbable victory.

**Internet Addresses**

http://www.superbowl.com/history/mvp/sbiii.html
http://www.profootballhof.com/famers/namath.html

**LYNN SWANN**

Shown here in his college days, Lynn Swann was known for making acrobatic catches.

**By the Time He Graduated** in 1974, Lynn Swann had 95 receptions, more than anybody else in the history of football at the University of Southern California. He was the school's third-best punt returner of all time.

Swann also earned a letter in track and field. He once long jumped 24 feet 10 inches. His best 100-yard dash time was 9.8 seconds.

In 1974, his rookie season with the Pittsburgh Steelers, Swann led the league with 577 punt-return yards. When the playoffs began, he had earned playing time as a wide receiver. In the AFC Championship Game, he caught a six-yard pass from Terry Bradshaw and scored, putting the Steelers ahead for keeps. Pittsburgh beat Oakland, 24–13.

Then in Super Bowl IX, Swann returned three punts for 34 yards. A 16–6 victory over Minnesota gave Pittsburgh its first title.

The 1975 season was another great year for Swann. He caught 49 passes for 781 yards and 11 touchdowns. But when he went up for a pass in the AFC Championship Game against Oakland, he was bashed in the head and knocked unconscious by a defender. That was his last play of the game; he spent two days in a hospital with a concussion, but Pittsburgh still prevailed, 16–10.

It looked like Swann's season might be over. With only two weeks until Super Bowl X, doctors told him he needed rest. On the day before the game he was finally able to practice, but he kept dropping passes.

Dallas safety Cliff Harris wondered if Swann would be tough enough to play. "Getting hit while he's running a route across the middle must be in the back of his mind," he said.[1] He hinted that Swann would be so scared of being hit again that he would not go for the ball.

The Pittsburgh star got mad. "He was trying to intimidate me," he said. "He said that I'd be afraid." Swann disregarded the doctors' advice and told his team, "I'm going to play."[2]

Dallas went ahead 7–0 when Roger Staubach hit Drew Pearson for 29 yards and a touchdown. A minute later Swann took off down the right sideline, chased closely by Cowboys cornerback Mark Washington. Bradshaw flung a pass at them; Swann reached inside Washington's arms to grab it just before he went out of bounds. "That catch seemed to boost me," he said. "I never had a day in my life when I felt so loose."[3]

Swann was not finished. In the second quarter, he was racing downfield when Bradshaw launched a bomb. Swann stumbled and the ball looked out of his reach. But he lunged and caught the 53-yard pass.

Despite Swann's heroics, the lead seesawed back and forth. Harris was still trying to play mind games with Swann. "Once, Harris . . . told me I was lucky because he'd just missed me with a hard shot," Swann remembered. "He said he was going to get me if I came across the middle."[4]

The Steelers were up 15–10 late in the fourth quarter when Bradshaw faded back and Swann went long. The Steelers quarterback released a pass just as he was clobbered by a Cowboys lineman. It was a beauty! The ball was caught by Swann as he raced by Washington. The play was good for 64 yards and a touchdown! Pittsburgh finally won the game, 21–17.

After the game, Harris did not have much to say. Washington said he would always remember trying to keep up with Swann: "It will take a lifetime to forget that day."[5]

# LYNN SWANN

BORN: March 7, 1952, Alcoa, Tennessee.

HIGH SCHOOL: Serra High School, Foster City, California.

COLLEGE: University of Southern California.

PRO: Pittsburgh Steelers, 1974–1982.

HONORS: Most Valuable Player, Super Bowl X; NFL 1970s all-decade team; Super Bowl silver anniversary team, 1990.

Lynn Swann makes a diving catch during Super Bowl X.

**Internet Address**

http://www.superbowl.com/history/mvp/sbx.html

TERRY BRADSHAW

Following his blockers, Steelers quarterback Terry Bradshaw tucks the ball and runs.

# TERRY BRADSHAW

**WHEN TERRY BRADSHAW JOINED** the Pittsburgh Steelers in 1970, they had never won any kind of title. In fact, the season before he arrived, they were 1–13. Eventually, he and teammates like running back Franco Harris, receiver Lynn Swann, and defensive lineman "Mean Joe" Greene turned the Steelers around.

After Bradshaw's fifth season, Pittsburgh had fought its way into Super Bowl IX against the Minnesota Vikings. In the fourth quarter with a slim 9–6 lead, Bradshaw directed a 66-yard drive that ended with a four-yard touchdown pass to Larry Brown. The Steelers won, 16–6. Harris, who ran for 158 yards, was named MVP.

The next year, Pittsburgh faced the Dallas Cowboys in Super Bowl X. Once again, the Steelers had a slight advantage, 15–10, in the fourth quarter. Bradshaw took the snap at his own 36-yard line and faded back, looking for receivers.

Bradshaw was about to be buried, but he kept looking downfield. Just as he let loose a bomb to Swann, Bradshaw was knocked cold by Larry Cole. Swann caught the pass and outran the Dallas secondary. Touchdown! Pittsburgh won 21–17, and Swann was named MVP.

The two teams met again in Super Bowl XIII. Bradshaw tossed a 28-yard scoring pass to John Stallworth. Soon after, Roger Staubach of the Cowboys hit Calvin Hill for 39 yards and a touchdown. Then Thomas "Hollywood" Henderson stripped the ball from Bradshaw. Mike Hegman scooped it up and ran 37 yards into the end zone. Dallas led, 14–7.

Bradshaw calmly connected again with Stallworth for a

75-yard TD. With twenty-six seconds left in the half, Pittsburgh regained the lead when he rolled out and tossed a four-yard scoring pass to Rocky Bleier. The Steelers were up, 21–14.

In the fourth quarter, Bradshaw underthrew a soft pass. Swann cut back to get it; he and cornerback Benny Barnes tangled feet as they fell to the turf. Swann held the ball and Barnes was called for interference. That took the ball to the Dallas 23-yard line. Two plays later, Harris picked up 22 yards and a touchdown.

The Cowboys fumbled the kickoff at their own 18-yard line. On the next play, Swann took off for the corner of the end zone where he caught a bullet from Bradshaw. Dallas scored two late touchdowns, but Pittsburgh won, 35–31.

Bradshaw finished the game with 318 yards while completing 17 of 30. This time he was the MVP.

The next year Pittsburgh again had to play catch-up in Super Bowl XIV. The Los Angeles Rams led 13–10 at halftime. In the third quarter, Bradshaw hit Swann for 47 yards and a touchdown. Pittsburgh now led the Rams, 17–13.

After Los Angeles regained the lead, Bradshaw threw two interceptions. The Rams seemed on the verge of an upset victory, but the veteran quarterback did what he had to do. A 73-yard bomb to Stallworth put the Steelers up for keeps. Harris recorded a one-yard scoring run that made the final score 31–19.

Bradshaw's final stats showed 14-of-21 completions for 309 yards. For the second year in a row, he was the game's MVP. At that point, he had thrown for more career touchdowns (9) and passing yards (932) than any other Super Bowl quarterback.

Bradshaw helped bring the Steelers into four Super Bowls—and they won every one of them! "I'll tell you this," he said. "We sure did hate to lose."[1]

# TERRY BRADSHAW

BORN: September 12, 1948, Shreveport, Louisiana.

HIGH SCHOOL: Woodlawn High School, Shreveport, Louisiana.

COLLEGE: Louisiana Tech University.

PRO: Pittsburgh Steelers, 1970–1983.

RECORDS: Shares NFL record for most Super Bowl wins as a starting quarterback, 4; holds postseason single-game record for highest average of yards gained per pass, 14.71; holds Super Bowl career record for highest average of yards gained per pass, 11.10.

HONORS: Most Valuable Player, Super Bowl XII, XIV; Associated Press regular season MVP, 1978; NFL 1970s all-decade team; elected to Pro Football Hall of Fame, 1989.

Bradshaw led the Steelers to four Super Bowl victories. In those four games, he combined to throw 8 touchdown passes.

**Internet Addresses**

http://www.superbowl.com/history/mvp/sbxiii.html
http://www.superbowl.com/history/mvp/sbxiv.html

MARCUS ALLEN

Breaking into the open field, Marcus Allen runs for the end zone.

THE RAIDERS OF THE 1980S WERE THE BAD BOYS of professional sports. They were loud, crude, and mean. They were also one of the best teams in the NFL. Even their owner, Al Davis, got into trouble. When he moved the team from Oakland to Los Angeles and back again in a span of thirteen years, the league took legal action against him.

Marcus Allen, the Raiders star running back, never seemed to fit in with the rest of the team. "He was soft-spoken, clean-cut, friendly—sort of a Mercedes among junkers," explained one sportswriter.[1]

Allen was already a star when he came to the Raiders. He had won the Heisman Trophy at the University of Southern California as the best college football player in the country in 1981. "He was a man," said his teammate Todd Christensen. "He might have been the toughest player I've ever been around, which is saying a lot for a running back."[2]

Allen was not just tough on the field. He worked hard to be one of the NFL's best running backs. Even in the off-season, he ran up steep hills to keep in shape.

In 1982, Allen carried the ball only 160 times, but he gained 697 yards and scored 11 touchdowns. However, the Raiders' season ended in the second round of the playoffs when they were beaten by the New York Jets, 17–14.

The next season, Allen's rushing total hit 1,014 yards. In the playoff opener, he scored twice, as Los Angeles beat Pittsburgh, 38–10. Then the team took apart Seattle, 30–14. Allen ran the ball 25 times for 154 yards and a touchdown.

That earned the Raiders a spot in Super Bowl XVIII

against the Washington Redskins, the defending champs. With Joe Theismann calling the signals and running back John Riggins chewing up the yards, the Redskins had beaten Miami, 27–17, in Super Bowl XVII. Going into the big game against Los Angeles, they had won 27 of their last 30 games.

Most sportswriters and fans expected a close, exciting game. The Raiders got lucky early when Derrick Jensen blocked a Washington punt and fell on it in the end zone for a touchdown. Steadily, Los Angeles built up a lead that was 21–3 at halftime.

In the third quarter, Allen put the game out of reach. On a first down from the Redskins 5-yard line, he took the handoff from Jim Plunkett. "The play . . . was designed to go to the right," said Christensen, "but Marcus saw an opening and just made an amazing cutback to his left . . . that, anatomically, he shouldn't have been able to do."[3] When he crossed the goal line, the Raiders led, 28–9.

On the last play of the quarter, Allen headed around the left end at his own 26-yard line. When he ran into a mass of Redskins, he turned around and headed back toward the other side of the field. After making it past the line, the field in front of him was clear, so he took off.

Only Anthony Washington was left to stop him. Receiver Cliff Branch raced downfield and bumped the defender aside. Allen zipped 74 yards into the end zone! With a full quarter left, the Raiders were trouncing the Redskins, 35–9.

When the game ended, it was 38–9, at that time the most points and the biggest margin of victory in Super Bowl history.

Allen's 191 rushing yards were another Super Bowl record. Amazingly, he had racked up that total with just 20 carries. That was an average of 9.6 yards per run.

## MARCUS ALLEN

BORN: March 26, 1960, San Diego, California.

HIGH SCHOOL: Abraham Lincoln Preparatory School, San Diego, California.

COLLEGE: University of Southern California.

PRO: Los Angeles Raiders, 1982–1992; Kansas City Chiefs, 1993–1997.

RECORDS: Holds Super Bowl record for the longest run from scrimmage, 74 yards; holds Super Bowl career record for highest average of yards gained per carry, 9.6.

HONORS: Heisman Trophy, 1981; Maxwell Award (outstanding college player), 1981; Most Valuable Player, Super Bowl XVIII; NFL Most Valuable Player, 1985.

At the time of his retirement, Marcus Allen held the NFL career-record for most rushing touchdowns.

**Internet Address**

http://www.superbowl.com/history/mvp/sbxviii.html

# DOUG WILLIAMS

Trying to move the ball down the field, Doug Williams looks to hit an open receiver.

# DOUG WILLIAMS

IN THE TWO WEEKS LEADING UP to Super Bowl XXII, Doug Williams just wanted to concentrate on preparing for the big game. However, the reporters wanted to talk about his race; Williams would be the first African-American quarterback to start in a Super Bowl.

Of course, for decades some of the National Football League's biggest stars had been African Americans, but very few had played quarterback. That position seemed to be reserved for white players.

Williams did not want to talk about his race. He was just happy that he and his team, the Washington Redskins, had earned a spot in the big game against the Denver Broncos. "If you're white, black, yellow, or pink, it means a lot to a quarterback, if you can take a team to the Super Bowl," he said.[1] His teammates did not seem to care about his color, either. "Black, white, green, yellow, we're going to win this thing with you," tackle Joe Jacoby told him.[2]

Then the day before the game, Williams had an emergency root canal operation. "I had trouble talking, but I went back to the hotel and laid down and watched TV and let the painkiller work."[3]

At first, the next day's game looked like a disaster for Williams and the Redskins. On the first play from scrimmage, John Elway hit Ricky Nattiel for 56 yards and a touchdown. Soon, a Rich Karlis field goal put the Broncos ahead, 10–0.

Meanwhile, the Redskins were going nowhere. The Washington receivers bobbled four passes. Then Williams dropped back to pass, slipped, and twisted his left knee. He tried to get up, but he collapsed and had to be helped to the bench. "I've played with pain before," he told Head Coach Joe Gibbs.[4] Then he limped back onto the field.

What happened next was the most incredible offensive explosion in the history of the Super Bowl. Ricky Sanders, Washington's star receiver, was supposed to go short for a quick hitch pass. When he was hit at the line, he took off. "All I had to do was put the ball in the air and he ran under it," Williams explained.[5] Eighty yards for a touchdown!

On the next possession, Williams saw receiver Gary Clark crossing to the left. He was open. "I threw the ball into the corner and he dove for it just over the goal line," remembered Williams.[6] Washington was on top, 14–10.

When linemen Jacoby and Raleigh McKenzie opened a big hole, Redskins running back Timmy Smith took the handoff and went 58 yards for a touchdown.

Then it was Sanders's turn again. "Ricky was several yards ahead of [Tony] Lilly when I hit him at the 10-yard line and he ran the rest of the way into the end zone."[7] The play covered 50 yards.

After Barry Wilburn intercepted an Elway pass, Williams was back on the field. A steady drive ended as he hit tight end Clint Didier for eight yards and another TD.

At halftime the Redskins led 35–10. They had scored 5 touchdowns on just 18 plays. "It was the greatest quarter of football I've ever been around," Gibbs said.[8] Until that day, no NFL team had ever scored 35 points in a quarter of a postseason game. After the half, Washington coasted to a 42–10 victory. Williams finished the game with 18 completions out of 29 attempts for 340 yards.

"I realize I am a role model," Williams said. "I feel very proud and very blessed. But the important thing was playing well and winning."[9]

# Doug Williams

BORN: August 9, 1955, Zachary, Louisiana.

HIGH SCHOOL: Chaneyville High School, Zachary, Louisiana.

COLLEGE: Grambling State University.

PRO: Tampa Bay Buccaneers, 1978–1982; Oklahoma Outlaws (USFL), 1984; Arizona Wrangles (USFL), 1985; Washington Redskins, 1986–1989.

HONORS: Most Valuable Player, Super Bowl XXII.

With Williams at quarterback the Redskins set a Super Bowl record for most points scored in a quarter.

**Internet Address**

http://www.superbowl.com/history/mvp/sbxxii.html

# Joe Montana

**His Come-From-Behind Victories** at Notre Dame earned Joe Montana the nickname "Comeback Kid." He led the Fighting Irish to a national title in 1977.

When he was a kid, Montana's hero was Joe Namath, who had turned the football world upside down at Super Bowl III. As a superstar with the San Francisco 49ers, Montana would make the Super Bowl the stage for his own incredible achievements.

An 11-yard touchdown pass to Earl Cooper and Montana's own 1-yard scoring run helped give the 49ers a 20–0 halftime lead over the Cincinnati Bengals in Super Bowl XVI. San Francisco held on to win, 26–21, and Montana was honored as the game's MVP.

In Super Bowl XIX, San Francisco fell behind 10–7. Then, Montana buried the Miami Dolphins with three second-quarter scoring drives. First, he hit Roger Craig with an 8-yarder, then he popped over the goal line himself from the 6. Finally, Craig scored on a 2-yard run.

When the dust cleared, the 49ers were victorious, 38–16. Montana had earned his second MVP award by throwing for 331 yards and three touchdowns—as well as running for 59 yards and another touchdown.

Jerry Rice, Montana's favorite receiver, had one of his greatest games in Super Bowl XXIII. He caught 11 passes, good for 215 yards. When Rice grabbed a 14-yard scoring pass early in the fourth quarter, the game was tied, 13–13.

But after the Bengals' Jim Breech kicked a 40-yard field goal, Cincinnati had a 16–13 lead with just 3:30 remaining. A penalty on the kickoff put the ball way back at the San

JOE MONTANA

Joe Montana made the most of his Super Bowl appearances. He led the 49ers to four titles, winning the MVP award three times.

Francisco 8-yard line. "We got 'em!" some of the Bengals began screaming. Cris Collinsworth was not so sure. "Will you see if number sixteen is in the huddle?" He was. "Then we haven't got 'em."[1]

Montana started the 49ers drive cautiously with three short passes to three different receivers. Then, he hit Rice for 17 yards and Craig for 13. The 49ers had a first down at the Bengal 35. The roar of the fans was almost deafening.

A penalty set them back ten yards, but then Montana sighted his man right over the middle. Rice was surrounded by three Bengals, but he went up and caught the ball. First down at the 18!

Montana and Craig connected for 8 more yards. With 39 seconds left, it was second down at the 10-yard line. For the big play, the Bengals expected Montana to go with the big man. When Rice went in motion, they focused on him. That left John Taylor open. The pass to Taylor was perfect. The 49ers won, 20–16.

Montana's last appearance in the Super Bowl came the next year against the Denver Broncos. When he showed up for the game, there was a photograph of his three children waiting for him. Each of them was wearing one of his Super Bowl rings. A message read, "OK, Daddy. The next ring is yours."[2]

Montana found Rice three times for touchdowns with passes of 20, 38, and 28 yards. He also had scoring tosses of 7 yards to Brent Jones and 35 yards to Taylor. San Francisco destroyed the Broncos, 55–10.

Montana had his fourth Super Bowl ring—and his third MVP award. After he threw for 297 yards and five touchdowns, there was no doubt.

Teammate Randy Cross said number sixteen was a very tough man to beat. "If every game was a Super Bowl," he said, "Joe Montana would be undefeated."[3]

# JOE MONTANA

BORN: June 11, 1956, Monongahela, Pennsylvania.

HIGH SCHOOL: Ringgold High School, Monongahela, Pennsylvania.

COLLEGE: University of Notre Dame.

PRO: San Francisco 49ers, 1979–1992; Kansas City Chiefs, 1993–1994.

RECORDS: Super Bowl career record for most yards passing, 1,142; Super Bowl single-game record for most yards passing, 357; shares Super Bowl record for most wins as a starting quarterback, 4; Super Bowl career record for highest passer rating, 127.8; Super Bowl career record for most completions, 83; Super Bowl career record for most touchdown passes, 11.

HONORS: Most Valuable Player, Super Bowl XVI, XIX, XXIV; named *The Sporting News* Man of the Year and Player of the Year, 1989; AP regular season MVP, 1989–1990; 75th Anniversary NFL all-time team, 1994; NFL 1980s all-decade team; elected to the Pro Football Hall of Fame, 2000.

In addition to his postseason success, Montana was named to play in the Pro Bowl eight times during his career.

**Internet Addresses**

http://www.superbowl.com/history/mvp/sbxvi.html

http://www.superbowl.com/history/mvp/sbxix.html

http://www.superbowl.com/history/mvp/sbxxiv.html

# EMMITT SMITH

**AFTER BEING ONE OF PRO FOOTBALL'S POWERHOUSE** teams in the 1970s, the Dallas Cowboys took a long, slow dive. In 1989, they were 1–15. Then, three men led one of the NFL's greatest turnarounds—Coach Jimmy Johnson, quarterback Troy Aikman, and running back Emmitt Smith.

Three years later, the Cowboys had battled their way into the NFC Conference Championship Game. Aikman completed 24 of 34 passes for 322 yards. Smith carried the ball 24 times for 114 yards. He scored on a 4-yard run and then on the receiving end of a 16-yard pass from Aikman. The San Francisco 49ers fell, 30–20, and Dallas was back in the Super Bowl for the first time in fourteen years.

Super Bowl XXVII was a joke—and the Cowboys enjoyed it immensely. The Buffalo Bills lost the ball nine times with 5 fumbles and 4 interceptions.

Smith had told reporters that he wanted to be the game's Most Valuable Player. Then, "in my first big run of the game, I went for 38 yards to their 19-yard line," he said. "But I wanted that touchdown badly. I still had my sights on the Super Bowl MVP."

He did not get it—even though he finally scored a touchdown and gained 108 yards. "Still," he admitted, "it's hard to compete with a guy who goes 22 of 30 for 273 yards and 4 TDs. Without a doubt, Troy deserved to be Super Bowl MVP."[1] Dallas demolished Buffalo, 52–17.

Because of a contract dispute, Smith missed the first two games of the 1993 season, and Dallas lost both of them. When he finally returned, the team posted an impressive

**EMMITT SMITH**

Running hard, Emmitt Smith breaks the tackle of Kenny Davidson of the Houston Oilers.

12–4 record. His 1,486 rushing yards led the league, and he was named the regular season MVP.

Once again, Dallas met San Francisco in the NFC Championship Game. Smith caught an 11-yard scoring pass and picked up 88 yards as the Cowboys cruised to a 38–21 triumph. "The key was Emmitt," said Dallas defensive coordinator Butch Davis. "He controlled the ball and kept us off the field."[2]

Then it was on to another battle with the Buffalo Bills. Super Bowl XXVIII was no blowout. The first time he carried the ball, Smith tried to jump over a tackler. Instead, Bruce Smith smashed into him and flipped him back. One of the Bills yelled, "Yeah! Yeah! It's gonna be like this all day!"[3]

At the half, Buffalo led, 13–6. "These boys came to play," exclaimed Cowboys receiver Michael Irvin.[4] In the locker room, Smith told the Dallas coaches, "I need the ball in my hands more. . . . Just get it to me."[5]

They did. On the first possession of the second half, Smith carried the ball on seven of eight plays for 64 yards. In the huddle, he yelled to his teammates, "Yeah! This is what I'm talking about! Give it to me again!"[6] A 15-yard run put him over the goal line. In the final quarter, he scored again on a one-yard gain.

When it was over, the Cowboys had rallied to beat the Bills, 30–13. Smith had gained 132 yards on 30 carries. He was named MVP.

After the game, Smith did not brag. In fact, he said he wished he could share the MVP trophy with safety James Washington, who had scooped up a fumble and ran 46 yards for the Cowboys' first touchdown.

He also gave lots of credit to his blockers. "The offensive line did a great job. They opened up holes for me to run the football."[7]

# EMMITT SMITH

BORN: May 15, 1969, Pensacola, Florida.

HIGH SCHOOL: Escambia High School, Pensacola, Florida.

COLLEGE: University of Florida.

PRO: Dallas Cowboys, 1990– .

RECORDS: NFL career record for most rushing touchdowns, 125; NFL single-season record for most touchdowns, 25; postseason record for most games over 100 yards rushing, 7; postseason record for most consecutive games over 100 yards rushing, 7; postseason career record for most touchdowns, 18; Super Bowl career record for most rushing touchdowns, 5.

HONORS: *The Sporting News* NFL Player of the Year, 1993; Most Valuable Player, Super Bowl XXVIII; *The Sporting News* Sportsman of the Year, 1994.

Smith won the MVP award for his play in Super Bowl XXVIII, but he also helped Dallas to victories in Super Bowl's XXVII and XXX.

**Internet Addresses**

http://www.superbowl.com/history/mvp/sbxxviii.html
http://www.nfl.com/players/profile/2961.html

TERRELL DAVIS

Busting through the line, Terrell Davis rumbles in for a touchdown against the Pittsburgh Steelers.

JOHN ELWAY KNEW that Terrell Davis, known as T. D., was just what the Denver Broncos needed. "Ever since his rookie season [1995], Terrell has taken the pressure off me to throw on every down," the veteran quarterback said. "Our offense has been better because people have had to worry about not only our passing game but also our running game."[1]

In only his second season, T. D. led the American Football Conference with 1,538 regular-season rushing yards. He did it again in 1997 with 1,750 yards and in 1998 with 2,008 yards. He had become only the fourth NFL player ever to surpass 2,000 yards rushing in a season.

It was in the postseason that Davis really got tough. In 1997, he blew open the wildcard match against Jacksonville with a 59-yard scoring run. Against Miami in 1998, he only carried the ball 21 times, but he gained 199 yards. A good chunk of that came on a 62-yard blast, the longest post-season run in Denver history.

Then T. D., Elway, and the Broncos found themselves in Super Bowl XXXII against the Green Bay Packers. It was Davis's first Super Bowl appearance, but Elway's fourth. The first three had all been losses, but this time the team was confident.

In the first quarter, his 1-yard touchdown run had given Denver a 7–7 tie. Then he was tackled by the Packers' Santana Dotson and Gilbert Brown. Soon he was on the sidelines, barely able to see. Right away, coach Mike Shanahan sent him back onto the field. "You don't have to worry about see-ing on this play because we're going to fake it to you."[2]

And so Davis quietly ran back onto the field. He took the fake from Elway, then was buried by the Green Bay line. Meanwhile, the quarterback snuck into the end zone. Denver led, 17–7.

Shanahan soon realized his star running back was in trouble. Davis was beginning to suffer from a headache so painful he was vomiting: "On came a raging, head-rattlin', mind-blowin' migraine."[3] Soon, he said, "instead of a football helmet, I was wearing an oxygen mask. Instead of taking handoff after handoff, I was taking deep breath after deep breath."[4]

For years, T. D. had suffered from terrible migraine headaches, but for many months, special medicine had helped prevent them. Unfortunately, with all the excitement of the Super Bowl, he had forgotten to take his pill! While his teammates battled the Packers, doctors gave him the medicine. Green Bay tightened the score to 17–14.

Slowly, his eyesight cleared and the pain disappeared. When the second half began, he was ready to play.

But on the first play, a pitchout from Elway, the ball slipped out of his hands and the Packers recovered. Soon they had a field goal and the game was tied 17–17.

Soon after a gutsy Elway run netted a first down at the Packer 4-yard line, Davis popped over the goal line from the 1. On that drive, T. D. had gained 21 yards. From then on, the Broncos were in charge. "Every time we ran the ball," Davis said, "we were getting big chunks of yardage."[5]

In the fourth quarter, Denver steadily moved downfield once again. Davis picked up his third touchdown of the day—a Super Bowl rushing record—on a 1-yard dash up the middle.

The Broncos took their first Super Bowl victory, 31–24. Davis, Elway, their teammates, and fans celebrated the biggest victory in the team's history.

# TERRELL DAVIS

BORN: October 28, 1972, San Diego, California.

HIGH SCHOOL: Abraham Lincoln Preparatory School, San Diego, California.

COLLEGE: Long Beach State University, Long Beach, California; University of Georgia.

PRO: Denver Broncos, 1995– .

RECORDS: Super Bowl single-game record for most rushing touchdowns, 3; shares Super Bowl single-game record for most points scored, 18; postseason career record for highest yards-per-carry average, 5.59.

HONORS: Most Valuable Player, Super Bowl XXXII; Associated Press regular season MVP, 1998.

Terrell Davis was fairly unknown to football fans when he was drafted in 1995. He quickly won a starting job with the Broncos, and gained 1,117 yards rushing during his rookie season.

**Internet Addresses**

http://www.superbowl.com/history/mvp/sbxxxii.html

http://www.nfl.com/players/profile/1538.html

# JOHN ELWAY

FOR A LONG TIME, the Super Bowl was a nightmare for Broncos quarterback John Elway.

Early in Super Bowl XXI, the Denver Broncos led the New York Giants, 3–0. The Giants went ahead with a touchdown. Then, Elway engineered a 58-yard drive that ended when he crossed the goal line himself from four yards out.

Early in the third quarter the Broncos had the ball first and goal at the 1-yard line. A goal line stand by the Giants seemed to fire them up. New York took control of the game and went ahead with 17 third-quarter points. Elway passed for 304 yards, but Denver lost 39–20.

The next year the Broncos met the Washington Redskins in Super Bowl XXII. "We know how to get here," Elway said. "Now let's find a way to win."[1] Instead it was Doug Williams and the Redskins who figured out how to win. After Denver jumped to a 10–0 lead, the Redskins buried the Broncos, 42–10.

Super Bowl XXIV was even worse. Joe Montana and the San Francisco 49ers destroyed Denver, 55–10. Elway was sacked four times and gave up a pair of interceptions. It got so bad that the 49ers' defense felt sorry for him. After knocking him down, linebacker Matt Millen helped Elway back up and whispered, "Hang in there. It's a tough one."[2]

It took the Broncos nine years to make it back to Super Bowl XXXII. With the score tied 17–17 late in the third quarter, the Broncos had third-and-6 at the Green Bay 12. Elway headed around the right end, but instead of running safely out-of-bounds, he tried to jump over Packers safety LeRoy Butler. He spun around, then landed at the 4-yard

JOHN ELWAY

John Elway won more games than any other starting quarterback in NFL history.

line for a first down. Terrell Davis said he knew Denver would win when John Elway "made like a helicopter and took to the air."[3]

After the big play, Elway jumped up and shook his arms in the air. After that, the inspired Broncos took control of the game. Denver beat Green Bay, 31–24.

In the celebration afterwards, Broncos owner Pat Bowlen yelled, "Just four words—This one's for John!"[4]

Davis hugged his quarterback and told him, "I'm so happy for you." Now nobody could say Elway could not win the big ones. "Tell me you're coming back next year."[5]

Many fans assumed that Super Bowl XXXII had been Elway's final game. After all, he was thirty-seven years old, one of the oldest players in the National Football League. And he finally had a Super Bowl ring.

But Elway decided he wanted another shot. He and the 1998 Broncos fought their way to Super Bowl XXXIII against the Atlanta Falcons.

Elway picked the Falcons tough defense apart. He alternated long and short passes to six different receivers. His longest was an 80-yard bomb to Rod Smith. When he was done, he had hit 18 of 29 passes for 336 yards. He also scored on a 3-yard draw play. Cameras caught him smiling at the bottom of the pile in the end zone.

He was still smiling when the game ended in a 34–19 Denver win. At thirty-eight, he was the oldest athlete ever to take MVP honors. "I never thought it could get any better than last year," he said. "I never, ever thought I would be the Super Bowl MVP."[6]

Three months later, Elway retired from professional football. "It's hard to walk away," he admitted. "I can't explain in words how much everyone has meant to me."[7] He was the first quarterback to leave the sport as a Super Bowl champion.

# JOHN ELWAY

BORN: June 28, 1960, Port Angeles, Washington.

HIGH SCHOOL: Granada Hills High School, Los Angeles, California.

COLLEGE: Stanford University.

PRO: Denver Broncos, 1983–1998.

RECORDS: NFL career record for most wins as a starting quarterback; Super Bowl career record for most passing attempts, 153; Super Bowl record for oldest player to ever score a touchdown.

HONORS: Most Valuable Player, Super Bowl XXXIII; Associated Press regular season MVP, 1987.

When Elway won the MVP award after Super Bowl XXXIII, he was the oldest player ever to receive that honor.

**Internet Addresses**

http://www.superbowl.com/history/mvp/sbxxxiii.html

# CHAPTER NOTES

## Bart Starr

1. Gene Schoor, *Bart Starr: A Biography* (Garden City, N.Y.: Doubleday & Company, Inc., 1977), p. 21.
2. Bart Starr, "Super Bowl I," *Super Bowl: The Game of Their Lives* (New York: Macmillan, 1997), p. 14.
3. Schoor, p. 9.
4. Ibid., p. 180.

## Joe Namath

1. Brad Herzog, *The Sports 100* (New York: Macmillan, 1995), p. 185.
2. Will McDonough, et al., *75 Seasons: The Complete Story of the National Football League, 1920–1995* (Atlanta: Turner Publishing, Inc., 1994), p. 207.
3. Herzog, p. 185.
4. "Namath's Guarantee," *Super Bowl Memories*, 1997, <http://www.nfl.com/history/memories/namath.html> (March 1, 1999).

## Lynn Swann

1. Phil Musick, "Super Bowl X," *The Super Bowl: Celebrating a Quarter-Century of America's Greatest Game* (New York: Simon & Schuster, 1990), p. 172.
2. Ibid., p. 176.
3. Ibid.
4. Ibid., p. 178.
5. Ibid.

## Terry Bradshaw

1. Phil Musick, "Super Bowl XIV," *The Super Bowl: Celebrating a Quarter-Century of America's Greatest Game* (New York: Simon & Schuster, 1990), p. 228.

## Marcus Allen

1. Jerry Green, *Super Bowl Chronicles* (Grand Rapids, Mich.: Masters Press, 1991), p. 229.
2. Todd Christensen, "Super Bowl XVIII," *Super Bowl: The Game of Their Lives* (New York: Macmillan, 1997), p. 249.
3. Ibid., p. 255.

## Doug Williams

1. Jerry Green, *Super Bowl Chronicles* (Grand Rapids, Mich.: Masters Press, 1991), p. 275.
2. Doug Williams, "Super Bowl XXII," *Super Bowl: The Game of Their Lives* (New York: Macmillan, 1997), p. 313.
3. Ibid., p. 309.
4. Green, p. 286.
5. Williams, p. 313.
6. Ibid.
7. Ibid., p. 314.

8. Shelby Strother, "Top of the Mountain, King of the Hill," *The Super Bowl: Celebrating a Quarter-Century of America's Greatest Game* (New York: Simon & Schuster, 1990), p. 346.

9. Ibid.

## Joe Montana

1. Mickey Herskowitz, "Super Bowl XXIII," *The Super Bowl: Celebrating a Quarter-Century of America's Greatest Game* (New York: Simon & Schuster, 1990), p. 357.

2. Roy Didinger, "Super Bowl XXIV," *The Super Bowl: Celebrating a Quarter-Century of America's Greatest Game* (New York: Simon & Schuster, 1990), p. 373.

3. Herskowitz, p. 360.

## Emmitt Smith

1. Emmitt Smith with Steve Delsohn, *The Emmitt Zone* (New York: Crown Publishers, Inc., 1994), p. 201.

2. David S. Neft, Richard M. Cohen, and Rick Korch, *The Sports Encyclopedia: Pro Football* (New York: St. Martin's Press, 1994), p. 692.

3. Smith, p. 253.

4. Neft, p. 693.

5. Smith, p. 256.

6. Ibid.

7. Neft, p. 693.

## Terrell Davis

1. John Elway, "Terrell Davis: An Appreciation," *TD: The Memoirs of the Denver Broncos' Terrell Davis* (New York: HarperCollins Publishers, Inc., 1998), p. x.

2. Terrell Davis with Adam Schefter, *TD: The Memoirs of the Denver Broncos' Terrell Davis* (New York: HarperCollins Publishers, Inc., 1998), p. 2.

3. Ibid., p. 5.

4. Ibid., p. 4.

5. Ibid., pp. 11–12.

## John Elway

1. Shelby Strother, "Super Bowl XXII," *The Super Bowl: Celebrating a Quarter-Century of America's Greatest Game* (New York: Simon & Schuster, 1990), p. 345.

2. Ray Didinger, "Super Bowl XXIV," *The Super Bowl: Celebrating a Quarter-Century of America's Greatest Game* (New York: Simon & Schuster, 1990), p. 374.

3. Terrell Davis with Adam Schefter, *TD: The Memoirs of the Denver Broncos' Terrell Davis* (New York: HarperCollins Publishers, 1998), p. 11.

4. Peter King, "This One's For John," *Sports Illustrated 1999 Sports Almanac* (New York: Little, Brown, and Company, 1998), p. 120.

5. Davis, p. 14.

6. Michael Silver, "The Magnificent 7," *Sports Illustrated*, February 8, 1999, p. 37.

7. "Elway Makes it Official," *Athlete Daily*, May 2, 1999, <http://www.athletedailycom/player/playe...1&SID=6010&personId=1062&articleId=31825> (August 12, 1999).

# INDEX